Dharmakaya

Dharmakaya

Paula Meehan

WAKE FOREST UNIVERSITY PRESS

Wake Forest University Press

This book is for sale only in North America.
Copyright © Paula Meehan, 2002
All rights reserved.

For permission, required to reprint or broadcast
more than several lines, write to:
Wake Forest University Press
Post Office Box 7333, Winston-Salem, NC 27109

Book designed by Richard Eckersley
Printed in the United States by Thomson-Shore
Text set in 11.5 point Enschedé Trinité
Library of Congress Control Number: 2001093243
ISBN (cloth) 1-930630-05-0
ISBN (paper) 1-930630-04-2

For Theo Dorgan

Dharma : Kaya – Truth : Body

There is nothing you can give a poet; nothing you can take away.

ANNA AKHMATOVA

When you got nothing, you got nothing to lose.

BOB DYLAN

At the actual moment of death, one has an overwhelming vision of Dharmakaya, or the Primary Clear Light of Pure Reality. It is as if the whole of existence suddenly appeared in its absolute totality and in an entirely abstract form . . . the Dharmakaya is identical with the experiencer's own consciousness, which has no birth and no death, and is by its very nature the Immutable Light.

STANISLAV GROF on The Tibetan Book of the Dead

Contents

Acknowledgements

Thanks to the editors of the following where some of these poems, or versions of them, were previously published or broadcast:

At the Year's Turning; BBC Radio 3 Postscript – *A Poem for Ireland*; *Caduceus*; *College Green*; *Finglas – A Celebration*; *Fortnight*; *The Gallery Press 25th Anniversary Celebration Booklet*; *The Irish Times*; *Last Words*; Lyric FM; *The New Shetlander*; *The Ogham Stone*; *Podium II*; *Poetry in Motion on the Dart*; *Poetry Instant – work by Noel Connor*; *Poetry Ireland Review*; *Poetry Now Anthology – Dun Laoghaire Rathdown 1997*, and *1998*; *Poetry Review*; *Portal*; *Recorder*; *The Stinging Fly*; *Transnational Literacy Seminar Handbook 1997*; *Verse*; *The White Page – An Bhileog Bhán*; *The Whoseday Book*; *Women's News*.

'The Lost Children of the Inner City' in a different version was the text for film *Alive Alive O*, Loopline Productions, 1999.

'Literacy Class, South Inner City' was commissioned by The National Adult Literacy Association.

Dharmakaya

Dharmakaya

for Thom McGinty

When you step out into death
with a deep breath,
the last you'll ever take
in this shape,

remember the first step on the street –
the footfall and the shadow
of its fall – into silence. Breathe
slow-

ly out before the foot finds solid earth again,
before the city rain
has washed all trace
of your step away.

Remember a time in the woods, a path
you walked so gently
no twig snapped
no bird startled.

Between breath and no breath
your hands cupped your own death,
a gift, a bowl of grace
you brought home to us –

become a still pool
in the anarchic flow, the street's
unceasing carnival
of haunted and redeemed.

The View from Under the Table

was the best view and the table itself kept the sky
from falling. The world was fringed with red velvet tassels;
whatever play ran in that room the tablecloth was curtains for.
I was the audience. Listen to me laughing. Listen
to me weeping. I was a child. What did I know?

Except that the moon was a porcelain globe and swung from a brass chain. O
that wasn't the moon at all. The moon was my true love. Oak was my roof and
under the table no one could see you. My granny could see me.
Out, she'd say. Out. And up on her lap the smell of kitchen and sleep.
She'd rock me. She'd lull me. No one was kinder.

What ails you child? I never told her. Not
one word would cross my lips. Shadows I'd say. I don't like the shadows.
They're waiting to snatch me. There at the turn of the stairs.
On the landing. To the right of the wardrobe. In the fridge, white ghosts.
Black ghosts in the coal shed. In the bread bin, hungry ghosts.

Somewhere, elsewhere, my mother was sulking in the rain. I call up
her young face. Who did she think she was with her big words
and her belt and her beatings? Who do I think I am to write her?
She must have been sad. She must have been lonely.
Discipline. Chastisement. I stretch out my four year old hands.

Fist

If this poem, like most that I write,
is a way of going back into a past
I cannot live with and by transforming that past
change the future of it, the now
of my day at the window watching
the coming and goings to Merrion Square,
then, when you present your hand to me
as fist, as threat, as weapon,
the journey back to find the hand of the little child,
the cupping of her balled fist
in my own two adult hands,
the grip of her fury, the pulse at her wrist
under the thin thin skin,
the prising loose of each hot finger
like the slow enumeration of the points of death
and the exact spot that I will have kissed
where the fate line meets the heart line –
my bloody mouth a rose suddenly blooming,
that journey takes all my strength
and hope, just as this poem does
which I present to you now.

Look! It's spread wide open in a precise
gesture of giving, of welcome,
its fate clear and empty, like the sky,
like the blue blue sky, above the square.

That Night There Was a Full Moon, Little Cloud

Granny's up late and she's hemming her shroud.
The run and fell of it, the seemingly
seamless kilter of the over halter
that she'll slap or dash, again biting in
with what's left of her teeth. After the tea
she'll read my leaves and though the voice falters
the vision's crystal. She knows my black sin

my deep delved delight in the self same
sin. I exult in it. A lump of coal
on a white linen tablecloth – *my soul:*
a picture of it, my granny says. My name

should be harlot or scarlet. I am doomed.
She sees. She tells me I am beautiful.
That I'll never have children, but a song
for every child I might have had and none
got easy but writ in the blood of men
who've displeased me. She swears it's true. No room
of my own till the grave. The moon's strong pull
will claim me as daughter. No blame. No wrong.

Take a breath. Hold it. Let it go.

The garden again. Finglas.
My younger sister on the coalshed roof playing circus.

Early June – elderblossom, sweet pea.
The morning carries the smell of the sea.

I'm above in the boxroom looking down at her
through the window. Eldest daughter

packing what will fit in a rucksack,
what of seventeen years I can hoist on my back.

I don't know where I'm going. She steps out
on the narrow breeze block fence. If I shout

I'll startle her. She'll fall.
I swallow back a warning, the call

of her name become a lump in my throat,
something stuck there all these years, a growth

I've tried to bawl out, dance out, weep.
The inarticulate foolish gestures of grief.

She falls anyway. I could not save her.
Then or now. My younger sister

stepping out, her tongue between her teeth,
a rapt concentration that stills the world beneath her feet.

I hold my breath. A sequinned leotard,
her velvet slippers, a cast-off battered

umbrella for balance. The spotlight blinds her,
the crowd is hushed, the tiger

paces his cage, the ringmaster
idly flicks at a fly with his whip. She falters.

I hold my breath. She finds her centre.
Then or now, I could not save her.

5

My Sister Lets Down Her Hair

into the winter bedroom and I turn
to the hollow of the bed we share,
her warmth still there and her smell.

It is coming on seven and she moves
by touch to her dressing. I know
every move of her and follow
her every move by the lamp of her golden hair.
As it was yesterday, and the day before,
so shall it be now in memory
a prayer for her going forth.

                    Back then,
we are lit in the cold morning by only
her rivery hair, the strong flow of her hair,
in the mirror her golden hair. The little
clouds of our breath eddy across the room
to the further shore of the window
giving on gardens and sheds. She keeps
an eye for the factory bus. Its lights
probing the room at last, she'll pick
up her bag and go from the house
without disturbing a soul.

I shift into her spot in the bed, an animal's lair,
lined with dreams and the smell of her hair,
till the dawn comes up with its clear, or its cloudy, light
wishing her back to haunt the day
with her rivery hair, her golden hair,
and I am any creature left for lonely.

The Lost Twin

My frail and breaking sister
I hold these memories in my aching arms.

Take them. I am not able
for them. I hand them on to you.

I have patched together
from hearsay, from family lore,

a quilt to cover you
against the coming winter.

    *

This is what came down to us: How our mother miscarried your twin
at the start of the second trimester. How she didn't know she was still
carrying you. How she thought it was indigestion . . . months later . . . the
surprise . . . when the doctor . . . emergency! emergency! The story grows.
I add her blue dress. The one with the chevrons. I have her sitting under
Nanny McCarthy's rose trellis. The pains beginning. The June sun hot on
her face. Sweating. Confused. I have reached so often across the years to
her outstretched hand. And pulled her to her feet and made the journey
with her.

    *

I sift for the grain of truth.
I winnow for what
I can verify with my own eyes.

Nanny McCarthy feeding you
with an eyedropper,
you swaddled in a drawer by the fire

though it was midsummer.
you born Gemini,
already undecided about whether to stay.

Someone saying –
They sent her home to die.

    *

7

I was three years old.
What could I know?
Except the grain of the wood
was the song of the coffin,
the knot in the wood,
your cry. Creature.

I think you were born lonely
to search the world wide
for your lost twin.

O once I'd a dream
of foetal heels hammering my head.
O once I'd a dream of falling
my hand slipping from your grasp

     *

And this memory. Not yours. Or anything to do with you. Mine. I show it
to you now. You don't have to carry it. Not the way I have. Leaving her that
last time. 'You'll never see me alive again.' She speaks calm and slow. A
statement of fact. No plea, no whine. June. My twentieth summer. I pick
up my rucksack and equally calm, equally slow, 'I don't care.'

I didn't. Not then. Not for many years after.

     *

And which self saved
at which self's expense?

     *

I'm putting down the globe.
I haven't the shoulders

to carry this cross,
to hold up this sky.

There is a particular guilt reserved
for children like us.

     *

Another memory. Hearsay! Hearsay! A thirteen year old girl, midsummer, a housing estate, eight o'clock in the evening, sweetpea and elderblossom, carries her drunken mother home from the pub. Piggy-back. Other children jeering. *Locked. Sloshed. Pissed. Paralytic.* And how sound travels, how it bounces off the cemented footpaths, the roadways, the pebbledashed façades, the hot metal of the neighbour's car. It is merciless in the sunshine.

*

It's been pass the parcel ever since.
I give it back to you now.
This medicine bundle.

This cure.
For loneliness. For abandonment.

My frail, my breaking sister,

when you look into
the beautiful and fearful
eyes of your own children,

and you open wide your arms

to leave them go, or leave them come
they'll surely read the history
of your lost twin.

There on your palm
they'll trace
through the dark and dangerous forest
the one path home to you.

Thunder in the House

was what my mother called the noise above
that shook the ceiling, made the windows hum,

not Jesus moving wardrobes, couches, beds –
shifting heaven's furniture to help his mam

when Jesus was a boy, not bold like us;
Was what she called the ructions in the flat above

when all hell broke loose, when for an hour
or two or three or four until he fell asleep

or headed out for more, we were the damned.
Fridays were the worst. He'd come in roaring.

She was curst and soundly whacked. Sometimes
we could even hear the individual smack

of his hand on her cheek. But rarely words. No.
Then when the door would slam: weeping.

I'd meet her sometimes on the stairs, bruised
black and blue or a stranger orange hue,

thick smeared panstick on her twelve year old face.
I thought she was like the coalman's mangy dog,

a sleeveen bitch so used to beatings she'd slither
at your ankles, belly low, waiting for the boot to drop.

She robbed me of my message money. A slide from my plait.
My blue scarf. I avoided her after that.

My mother had no answers, or if she knew,
was leaving well enough alone. My own father

got cranky and threatened to settle his hash. God
love her, they'd say, she has nobody else. It'd go

even harder on her if anyone interfered.
She disappeared one cold midwinter's day,

the year I lost faith in Santa, though I stood
scanning Gardiner Street all Christmas Eve,

the bulletins shouted back to the younger kids –
a glimpse of his hood between chimneys, a snatch of red –

with thunder in the house, and shiny rain on all the roads
while from our plastered ceiling shook a fine fall of snow.

My Father's Hands That Winter

That year there was cold like no other winter.
Every morning
going out was a gymnastic affair.

Even the steps inside
the house, nearly to the door
of our flat on the third floor, were iced

over. Mrs Mac broke a leg
and Harry Styx (for the first time in his life he said)
found it much too hard to beg.

We became technicians of the slide
and forward propulsion,
of throwing your body, arms wide

open, out into some zone of contract
with the air, where coming to a stop
ever ever again was taken on trust.

The city looked good enough to eat
and *weathervane* was a new word
I picked up from a storybook. Our feet

were always wet and numb and blue.

                    *

It's why I remember my father's hands so clearly.
He was out of work. It must have been through

desperation on the cusp of Christmas that he took
a job in Carton's as a turkey plucker.
For buttons, he said, and I saw a frock

like the girl's in the storybook, all fuddy duddy
in ribbons and flounces with black patent shoes.
His hands were swollen, scratched raw and bloody

from the sharp ends of feather, of sinew,
of tendon, from the fourteen-hour day,
from the bite of the boss. At the window

I'd watch each morning, impatient for dawn
and ice engineering. He'd boil up
a big pot of eggs, school lunch for us children.

He'd button down the younger ones' coats
gingerly, and tie up the laces of their shoes
and tuck in our scarves at our delicate throats

– an egg in each pocket to keep us warm,
old socks on our hands to guard against chilblains.
A kiss on his forehead to keep him from harm.

    *

The city must have thawed at last
and unmagicked that winter when
I reached the age of reason. The past

was a new territory I would explore
at leisure and at will
by pushing on the unlatched tenement door.

I could hold in mind forever now
my father's hands that winter and
the city walls and railings freaked with snow.

The Exact Moment I Became a Poet

for Kay Foran

was in 1963 when Miss Shannon
rapping the duster on the easel's peg
half obscured by a cloud of chalk

said *Attend to your books, girls,*
or mark my words, you'll end up
in the sewing factory.

It wasn't just that some of the girls'
mothers worked in the sewing factory
or even that my own aunt did,

and many neighbours, but
that those words 'end up' robbed
the labour of its dignity.

Not that I knew it then,
not in those words – labour, dignity.
That's all back construction,

making sense; allowing also
the teacher was right
and no one knows it like I do myself.

But: I *saw* them: mothers, aunts and neighbours
trussed like chickens
on a conveyor belt,

getting sewn up the way my granny
sewed the sage and onion stuffing
in the birds.

Words could pluck you,
leave you naked,
your lovely shiny feathers all gone.

The Lost Children of the Inner City

MOLLY MALONE

Out of the debris of history
a song, a name,
a life we piece together

from odds and ends,
the cast off, the abandoned,
the lost, the useless, the relicts.

She died of a fever
the urge to save her
the same urge to gather

up the broken and the maimed
and what remains
after: a song, a name

and tokens of the sea
salty as life blood, as tears
she is moved to

though cast in bronze now
her unafflicted gaze
on the citizens who praised her

and raised her aloft
who are blind as her own bronze eyes
to the world of her children.

Pray for us who have lost our wings
Pray for us who are broken

Pray for us whose children are cold under clay
Or swept to sea on the wind

Pray for us who live in darkness
Pray for us who die in darkness

Our children were our song
Our song is over

We are dumb with grief
Pray for us who have lost our wings

Somewhere in the stone
was a smile, a curious gaze;

somewhere in the stone
was a human face;

somewhere in the stone
was a wink and a nod;

somewhere in the stone
was the labourer and the hod.

The mason found the gesture
like the sky when dark finds a star.

HISTORY LESSON

We read our city like an open book –
who was taken and what was took.

Spelt out in brick and mortar,
a history lesson for every mother's daughter.

Who owns which and who owns what?
The devil owns the bleeding lot!

GRANDMOTHER, GESTURE

My grandmother's hands come back to soothe me.
They smell of rain. They smell of the city.

They untangle my hair and smooth
my brow. There's more truth

to those hands than to all the poems
in the holy books. Her gesture is home.

The lines on her palms are maps:
she makes the whole world up –

she disappears it. It sings for her.
Its song is water, the sky is its colour.

She unpicks all riddles and solves
the small mysteries. She keeps the wolves

from the door. She opens wide the door.
Summer comes spilling in with a roar.

WINDOW ON THE CITY

If you blink you'd miss it,
your own life passing
into memory, frame by frame.

Sometimes you can't be sure of your own name.
So fast, the changing
face of the city. From where you sit

not the swish of the tyger's tail,
not the twitch of the tyger's whiskers
not a glance of his frisky eye

regarding: just the emptiest sky,
pockets that couldn't be any lighter,
a train singing on its iron rail.

BUDDLEJA

Self-seeding, stubborn, cute,
given half a chance they root

in a hair's breadth gap in a brick,
or chimneypot. Or fallen into a crack

and left for a year they're a shrub
tough and tenacious as your indigenous Dub.

When they break into blossom – so free, so beautiful.
I name them now as flags of the people.

Ectopic

The four full moons of the yellow sky
pulsate. Four full moons and I need
morphine. I need more morphine to stop the hurting.

I would gut my granny for another hit.
Someone's sewn me up and left the kitchen tap,
the Apple Mac, a rabid bat, a handy anvil

inside me. The stitches there above the mons
(*Won't interfere with the bikini line...*) neat
as my own white teeth clenched and grinding in pain,

that grin up, second mouth!, at the ceiling lights, the moons! and
I will work out their complicated orbits
relative to the sun and why the stars have

all deserted me. I want to know the weight
of my little creature's soul and why its fate

has been to leave before I had a chance to save
her. Or him. It? They keep calling it *it*.
I am a woman with a sieve carrying sand

from the beach. And all this time the rain
is hammering the window pane. I count perfect feet.
Your ten perfect toes. Your perfect fingers ten. Your blue eyes, since,

perfect foetus, I must summon the will to kill
you soon before you get too strong a grip
on the black hole that occupies the void that was my heart.

O somewhere there is a beautiful myth of sorting,
of sifting through a mountain of dross to find the one seed
whose eventual blossom is such would make a god cry.

Train to Dublin

I lay my head on Akhmatova's lap,
sob like a child, thumb in my mouth.
She sings me lullabies, eases me into the dark.

Mother of my spirit, my guide,
sweet lady smelling of mint and apple,
I lay my head on Akhmatova's lap

and sleep. This night the train will reach
the city. I'll find my healer.
I lay my head on Akhmatova's lap.

At dawn the red fox passed my gate,
the swallows came back to Eslin,
the willow sighed at my leaving.

I took my poems and passport;
my sister's gold ring in my ear,
walked into my fate in the clothes on my back.

I lay my head on Akhmatova's lap and
sob myself to sleep. I'll
wake to song, a whorl

of light and your face
coming towards me out of a dream.
I lay my head on Akhmatova's lap.

Mayday

Three Love Songs

THE COAST OF LEITRIM

On an autumn day in the hot city
blue sky and black shadow cast
to concrete and grey sward and dust, a lost
voice urges leave all the pretty

people behind, spend this equinox
walking the long and lonely coast of Leitrim.
You come too. Do. On a whim.
The way you used to, intox-

icated with me and my other, ready
to hop on a bus or a plane or a train or
any craft to share the transport, before
we grew serious and dour. *Steady,*

steady, you'd say as our heads blew off
or the sea dissolved another cliff face
or a fissure opened and swallowed us
whole. Because, my honey, you'd have to laugh

at how little stays the same. Grown
up now and no wiser than that first
time we walked the coast of Leitrim, no worst
there was none . . . so delicate and unknown

to each's other, finding my own lovely coastline
as exotic as the unmapped edge of the universe
that expands rapidly to leave way too much space
between our stars. Littorally fine

as when you reached for my hand
that day, at the sea's restless edge.
In sight of two rivers you solemnly pledged
my kingdom was as much land

as I could walk: the whole coast
of Leitrim – each rock and stone of it, each cloud,
each water-loving willow and every common herb, each blade
of grass, and even every shadow that they cast.

The first time I cross the Bog of Moods
I misread the map.
The Bog of Moons I thought it was
and watched as your white cap

lifted by a sudden squall
was cast before me into the canal
a full moon itself on the jet black water
shattering the perfect mirror

of the starry heavens. Seeds
of light prolific as common duckweed,
fen sedge, pollution-intolerant arrowhead.
Bistort. Bulrush. Bog Bean. Bur-reed.

The low down belly rooted naming
of these wet toed, turf sucking
mockers at our hamfisted, clubfooted clumsy
taking of each other. Glory be to whimsy

and misreading that have us cross the Bog
of Moots or Moos. For yes, they're there –
the slow moan of them squelching through the fog
of their own breaths, swinging full udders,

dainty hoofs picking through bladderwort
and crowfoot. Hells bells! And helleborine!
The harder you look, the more you will have seen;
and I say forgive me for the tense and curt

way I've been all day. The world
had shrunk to the proportion of the narrowboat.
I was a termagant curled
in the prickly armour of my pre-menstrual overcoat

barking at the moon, the mood,
the moot, the moos, until the moment when we stood
hand in hand under the stars and you showed me the rare
and lovely Grass of Parnassus, far

from its usual habitat. And something loosened
and came right, as if the land
herself was settling down, plumping out her skirts,
prepared to take her ease, and done with birth.

AT SLYGUFF LOCK

You whisper sweet nothings to my chilled ear.
The boat rocks; the wind swings round the compass
and drops the wild plums to the ground. I fear
the storm will break the ties and turn us loose

on the river's floodwater that carries
wrenched trees; galvanised sheets; plastic bottles;
one sheep's carcass, its face full of worries.
You ask I listen – the river's glottals

in duet now with canalwater's fall.
It drowns out even my own heart thumping,
the thock of the boat on the granite wall,
the insidious *chunka* of chains bumping.

All this to do about nothing, sweetheart.
With each falling leaf, a spark of god'sfire
singeing the earth where it falls. O the chart
to these waters says nothing about air

(for its long repeat makes the pattern hard
to map), and water is faster than stone,
and mountains are slowest of all – they ward
off the fickle, the inconstant. They hone

themselves in pure air, which element tonight
is ours to shine in, while the river sobs
its long song of courtship to the moon's bright
face; sheltering near us, a swan and her cob.

The Tantric Master

For I shall consider his beautiful navel firstly
– an altar! – whereat I've often offered flowers,
the yellow buttercup especially, a monstrance I can elevate
to the memory of his mother who surely taught him to pet.
And honeysuckle and meadowsweet and the wild dog rose:
one for its scent, one for its sound, and one for the tone of his skin
that is all petal to me.
                    For I shall consider
secondly each individuated pore of his entire body
and consider each at length having nothing better
to do with my time, and each being a universe unto itself.
This I call rapture.
                    And thirdly, to make no bones
about it, being the crux, the hardest part of the matter,
I shall consider his noble and magical wand. He do good
business throughout the night with it. He enchant,
and spellbind and wind me round his little finger;
or, on a moony night in April, even his little toe.

Which brings me to his nails: he keepeth that trim and smooth
the better to pleasure me. So subtle his touch I can feel
the very whorls of his fingerprints and could reconstruct from memory
his mark on my breast. Each ridge the high mountain,
each trough the deep canyon, unfathomable;
but I, having buckets of time, do fathom, do fathom.

For I shall consider the mesmeric draw of his nipples,
like standing stone circles on the broad plain of his chest,
megalithic power spots when I lay my hot cheek
on the cool of his belly and sight through the meadows
and the distant forests the trajectory of sun and other stars.

His mouth, I won't go into, being all cliché in the face of it,
except to say the dip of his lip is most suited to suction and friction,
and other words ending in tion, tion, tion which come to think of it
when I'm in the grip of it, is exactly how I make sweet moan.
                    For I shall consider
him whizzbang dynamo and hellbent on improving my spiritual status.

You can keep your third eyes and your orbs sanctimonious
the opening of which my Master believes *is* the point.
He says I'm a natural and ultimate enlightenment a mere question of time.
But in patient devotion I'll admit to deficiency. The theory of being
not a patch on just being is. Yap I distrust! Show me.
Don't tell me the way. The right place for talk of this ilk
is not during, not after, and foretalk will get you nowhere at all.
The best that I hope for in our daily instructions
is the lull between breaths, spent and near pacified.

Elder

I love its fecundity, its left alone
self designing wildness, especially in June,
the tomcat pungency of elderblossom
reeking in our rooms.

Six foot a year the thicket spread.
The Last of the Dublin Rain Forest you dubbed
it, and I am glad I can't
get my green hands on the garden below. I content

myself with windowboxes and the tops of wardrobes.
I feel like a cliff dweller, three floors up,
and fantasize a rope ladder to access potherbs
for the bitter cup

I'm wont to make for you: of red valerian
and stinging nettle - sleeping draught,
blood purifier. But this inebriation
of elder has me driven daft,

as if I've taken a secret lover,
a night tyger,
and you might come home early from the deeps
to find his paw prints on the sheets.

Aubade

I want to hold you dream-fast
for a spell,
time at least to tell
you clear I *love you* morning sudden as a bell-
note cast
this leaden clouded dawn
before you fall out with a sleep-shucking yawn
from the tangled damp lawn
bedsheet, scattering dustmotes, unshackled at last.

Your hands at rest, your breath calm.
You are drift-
wood, your self a gift
that's washed I *love you* clear of water in the lift –
wave psalm
of passion's break with dark
which covenants in the hard earned holy ark
that the day begins. Mark
this uncharted, unknown territory. Your palm

is cupped to catch the first light.
Soon I'll scry
future, past, and why
now is I *love you* pouring; grief-laden the sky.
Last night
the pain was signalled clear:
your back against me, you wouldn't let me near
you. No word, no touch. Fear
ruled our bed: new love flying its name, a black kite.

Manulla Junction

after a photograph by Father Browne

She stands in the station the first day of spring
halted forever in that precise gesture. Something
fey to this girl, with her father's old suitcase
tied up with twine. The wind in her face,

the wind in her golden hair, all of Irish history at her back,
no notion of what might lie further on down the track.
The taste of the unknown city on her tongue,
or a song she has never heard sung

which torments her and turns her narrow bed
into a grave. Or is this what I choose to read and have read?
Why such a lonely narrative? Why not
a joyous journey ahead of her to a glorious spot?

Why assign her victim? Why deduce grief
from her shiny shoes, from the fresh budded leaf?
What drew Father Browne to her radiant face –
the still centre of the photo – draws me too, intense

focus for the drama of the shot,
energy radiating outward from her now bleached face. Not
that she's aware of him or his camera
still less posterity's gaze that recruits her to my opera.

I want to give her a happy ending. Or
at least like me a path she can endure.
O save her god of twisty and already written fates
from unfordable rivers and padlocked gates,

with a goodbye to the chickens, the haws and the rain
crying down on the roof, the broken pane,
the rattling latch, the morning she woke to and rose to and went
from out her father's house, those angers spent.

Suburb

DESIRE PATH

For days before the kids were gathering stuff –
pallets and cast-off furniture, the innards of sheds,
the guts of Barna huts. Local factories on red alert
for raiding parties under cover of dark.

I watched them lug and drag fair-got and knocked-off
gear across the park, to the gap in the hedge,
to their deep ditched hoarding spot where they kept
it dry and guarded against the rival gang's attack.

They reminded me of bees, making to the flower,
or worker ants. Their comings and goings wore

the grass away until there was only bare earth
on their preferred track – a desire path

inscribed on the sward. I reckon seen from above
it must look umbilical to some object of exotic love.

STOOD UP

Leaning against the tree for over an hour,
young man waiting – for his girl, I assume.
All Souls' Day and the leaves falling dreamily.
I've seen the girl he's waiting for, a flirt,

up at the pub with the shiny gang, a short time
ago. Skulling pints. She's having a baby.
At least that's the word out there on the street.
They say it's not his. The first day of winter

is sweet and mild and gold and blue. He looks
beyond the aspen's tremulous leaf
to where small children fan the embers

of last night's bonfire. They coax a flame. It sucks
the air vigorously, then hesitates, then takes like grief
that's easier borne now than it will be to remember.

PYROLATRY

'Our wheelie bin was missing after the bin collection today.
It has No. 13 painted in white on one side.
If you happen to see it, please let us know.'
Should I tell them about the flames I saw

earlier – the green and the purple and the blue. The way
they snaked and writhed, sometimes narrow, sometimes wide,
could only have been plastic, toxic and noxious, so
strong the smell on the breeze. I had to claw

the washing in, which hung for hours in Virgo
from the drying line, which reeled and jigged
through that constellation until dark fell

and the wind dropped its poisoned cargo.
The flames veered east, then north, the kids ligged
round; then someone turned up with a drum – autumn's knell.

STINK BOMB

The smell of which still hangs about the house
despite the scented candles, the essential oils
I've burned and censered through the rooms
like a priestess in a diabolic rite.

Of course the row we had could have roused
the undead and the dead alike. It left me coiled
in a foetal crouch behind the couch, some womb
I was trying to get back to. And shite

if we didn't wake next door's dog; the Hound from Hell
Himself right on cue. You'd have to laugh. Or die
trying. Between your irrefutable logic

and my inarticulate sobs, we missed the door bell
ringing, we missed the children singing trick
or treat, trick or treat, the ghost afloat, the witch afly.

MISTLE THRUSH

The sycamore is weeping leaves of fire;
a maple stands in its own flaming lake;
shy birches isolate in yellow puddles.
You'd half expect these young trees to kick

their fallen skirts away. Bride? Bullfighter?
Dervish dancer rapt in a swirling cape?
When I went out an hour ago to muddle
through the leafdrift at my door, a flock

of mistle thrush descended – a deputation
from the wingéd world with urgent and with fatal news:
Dying is simple. You breathe in, you breathe out, you breathe in,
you breathe out and you don't breathe in again.
They acted like this was cause for celebration
– the first minor chord of my winter blues.

SUDDEN RAIN

I'm no Buddhist: too attached to the world
of my six senses. So in this unexpected shower,
I lift my face to its restorative tattoo,
the exultation of its anvil chime on leaf.

On my tongue I taste the bitter city furled
in each raindrop; and through the sheeted fall of grief
the glittery estate doth like a garment wear
the beauty of the morning; the sweet reek of miso

leached from composting leaves. Last night's dream
of a small man who floated in the branches of an oak
harvesting mistletoe with a golden sickle

I intuit as meaning you'll be tender and never fickle
this winter, though this may be synaesthetic
nonsense; I've little left to go on, it would seem.

Her tongue would flense the flesh from off your back.
I've never heard her utter a good word
about a neighbour or a friend in need.
Yet half the time you'd listen to spite your self,
knowing full well tomorrow it's your turn
to squirm and be lambasted on the spit,
the faggots stacked about your feet, the match

struck and held to straw and twigs. Should it catch
and take – the whole estate is lit
in the glare and glamour, while the one who burns
discovers the heft of our black craft, our art, frail shell.
Each flaming word a falling leaf – seed
nurturer and comforter that'll one day lift a bird
from the earth to its nest, a worm in its beak.

Literacy Class, South Inner City

One remembers welts festering on her palm.
She'd spelt 'sacrament' wrong. Seven years of age,
preparing for Holy Communion. Another is calm
describing the exact humiliation, forty years on, the rage

at wearing her knickers on her head one interminable day
for the crime of wetting herself. Another swears she was punch drunk
most her schooldays – clattered about the ears, made to say
I am stupid; my head's a sieve. I don't know how to think.

I don't deserve to live.
                            Late November, the dark
chill of the room, Christmas looming and none of us well fixed.
We bend each evening in scarves and coats to the work
of mending what is broken in us. Without tricks,

without wiles, with no time to waste now, we plant
words on these blank fields. It is an unmapped world
and we are pioneering agronomists launched onto this strange planet,
the sad flag of the home place newly furled.

The Trapped Woman of the Internet

She turns to me or any other watcher
her freaked almond eyes: I imagine she says
rescue me, rescue me. And the only
rescue I can mount is to shift website
from Asiatic Babe Cutie Triple XXX Sexpot.
        Yet much as I want I cannot leave her
rest. She bothers me all the mundane livelong day.
I carry her to the edges of my own lonely
room, and in the coldest hour of this winter's night
I lay her down upon a fragrant cot

        of dried meadow grasses, strewing herbs;
and off her thin and pallid face
I sponge the thick and viscid stuff;
        and at this point before the fire, I have to curb
such useless gesture towards an empty space
where no one can be saved, or loved enough

to save ourselves from our own virtual childhoods,
to puzzle ourselves free from those enchanted woods.

Swallows and Willows

When he caught me at the corner
with the curly headed green eyed boy
he brought me into detention.

'Write out, let me see,
a verse of a poem. Any
verse of your choice,

but longer than a quatrain,
five lines at least.
A hundred times.'

     from The Jailer (underlined three times)
     by Sylvia Plath

          I imagine him
          Impotent as distant thunder,
          In whose shadow I have eaten my ghost ration.
          I wish him dead or away.
          That, it seems, is the impossibility.

I was neat at first, maybe
neat to the tenth time, then
a looping downward scrawl.

Out the window – swallows
and willows and sun on the river.
'I meant a verse from a *set* text.'

I sat at the edge of his class
right into summer exams
sulky, and lonely, and cruel.

In Memory, John Borrowman

All things move through me:
the wind that shakes the willow;
my old friend's last breath.

On Poetry

for Niamh Morris

VIRGIN

To look back then:
one particular moon snared in the willows
and there I am sleeping in my body,
a notebook beside me with girl poems in it
and many blank pages to fill
and let there be a rose and the memory of its thorn
and a scar on my thigh where the thorn had ripped

earlier that day in the abandoned garden
where he came first to me
and lifted my skirt
and we sank to the ground.

And let me be peaceful
for I wasn't.
Not then, nor for many moons after.

mother you terrorist
muck mother mud mother
you chewed me up
you spat me out

mother you devourer
plucker of my soul bird
mammal self abuser
nightmatrix huntress

mother keeper
of calendar and keys
ticking off moon days
locking up the grain

mother house and tomb
your two breasts storing
strontium and lies
when you created time

mother you created plenty
you and your serpent consort
you and your nests
you and your alphabets

mother your pictographs
your mandalas your runes
your inches your seconds
your logic your grammar

mother wearing a necklace of skulls
who calls into being
by uttering the name
mater logos metric

mother your skirts
your skins your pelts
with your charms
old cow I'm your calf

mother fetishist
heart breaker
forsaker and fool
in the pouring rain

mother I stand
over your grave
and your granite headstone
and I weep

WHORE

I learnt it well. I learnt it early on:
that nothing's free, that everything is priced
and easier do the business, be cute, be wized
up and sussed, commodify the fun

than barter flesh in incremental spite
the way the goodwives/girlfriends did
pretending to be meek and do as bid
while close-managing their menfolk. It wasn't right.

I believed it wasn't right. See me now –
I'm old and blind and past my sexual prime
and it's been such a long and lonely time
since I felt fire in my belly. I must allow

there'll be no chance of kindling from my trance
the spark that wakes the body into dance;
yet still comes unbidden like god's gift: an image –
a boy turns beneath me, consolatory and strange.

Thaw in Milford, Michigan

for Thomas Lynch and Mary Tata

This year I do not feel it in my bones –
the spring return – but by an act of will
or faith believe it so. The low moan
of doves in magnolia, the ice from the windowsill
frittering, drips on a rusty tin all night
and under last autumn's leaves the green nubs of daffodils
pushing: signs I put together. But
something's locked, or frozen, wintering still,

inside me where it matters most. The heart
maybe, old site of anguish and remorse.
And not your voice irrupting, in love for the most part,
into this room, but kindness too, a clear force
for goodness, down the line from Dublin, and not
your shadow cast through the March evening of our flat,

nor even your desire stirring in the song you sing
me down the line, has power to shift what feels like stone
from the pre-resurrectionary tomb. Whatever's in the offing
bides its time and chooses it. No one
knows it better than we do: the holding firm,
in doubtful or in adverse seasons, to a sure belief
that poems will come again, and when they come
will scour the silted snowbanks of the street, and loose our grief.

Recovery

The gardener is sweeping
the moss garden free
of the fallen husks of moss blossom
and other debris

that the wild wind dumped on it.
Such careful work
on such a small scale.
She loosens up the rich loam with a fork.

Her brow bowed to the ground
down on her knees there –
no time, and all time
to work this gently on the earth.

I have been bad all winter
and dreamt through last night's bitter cold
that this is my final spring –
the first green still cased in gold.

The gardener is so delicate,
each gesture a sure touch,
as if she were painting a miniature landscape
with her bristle brush.

I could watch her forever
at her patient sweeping.
Across the valley, in the state forest, the crew
are trail blazing.

Though I cannot see them
I have heard since dawn
at the very edge of my world
the whine of their machines.

I want to be like her. To take care
of the garden, to sweep clear a bed
of the deepest, greenest moss,
to recover a mossy pillow for my weary head.

It Is All I Ever Wanted

for Eavan Boland

to sit by this window
the long stretched light of April falling
on my desk, to allow

the peace of this empty page
and nearing
forty years of age

to hold in these hands
that have learnt to be soothing
my native city, its hinterland

and backstreets and river scored
memory of spring
blossom and birds –

my girl-poems
fountaining
over grief and the want of someplace to call home.

Last week I took as metaphor, or at least as sign,
a strange meeting:
a young fox walking the centre line

down the south side of the Square
at three in the morning.
She looked me clear

in the eyes, both of us curious
and unafraid. She was saying –
or I needed her to say – *out of the spurious*

the real, be sure
to know the value of the song
as well as the song's true nature.

Be sure, my granny used to say,
of what you're wanting,
for fear you'd get it entirely.

50

Be sure, I tell myself,
you are suffering
animal like the fox, not nymph

nor sylph, nor figment,
but human heart breaking
in the silence of the street.

Familiar who grants me the freedom of the city,
my own hands spanning
the limits of pity.

A Woman's Right to Silence

When the silence of the grave
steals over me as it does
like a mantle that comforts each day

I fancy it could save
me, the way the fuzz
on a sweet peach, say

the one you gave
me in bed not an hour ago nuzz-
ling up and making even the grey

of this spring morning easier to bear
can save me; or those first
ash leaves that as I decide

which skirt to wear
start their slow deliberate burst-
ing from the bonny black bead,

allow me claim silence as a rare
and fine sister, not in the least a curst
state, but ecstatic, free, untried.